PLANET EARTH

Coastlines
Volcanoes
The Oceans
Water on the Land
The Work of the Wind
Weather and Climate
Glaciers and Ice Sheets
Vegetation
Mountains and Earth Movements
The Solar System

First published in 1984 by
Wayland (Publishers) Ltd
49 Lansdowne Place, Hove
East Sussex BN3 1HF, England

© Copyright 1984 Wayland (Publishers) Ltd

ISBN 0 85078 381 X

Phototypeset by
Direct Image, Hove
Printed in Italy by
G. Canale & C.S.p.A., Turin
Bound in the UK by
R.J. Acford, Chichester

PLANET EARTH

VEGETATI

David Lambert

Contents

Plants grow in many shapes and sizes, each adapted to the climate it lives in.

Prehistoric plants

The world wears a cloak of living green. Vegetation springs up wherever it is moist and warm enough for plants to grow. Only the very coldest and driest lands lack any covering of plants. Plants also flourish in the sea. Billions upon billions of tiny plants drift in its surface waters.

Plants matter more to us than many of us realize. Green plants produce the oxygen we need to breathe, and all animals, including man, depend on plants for food at first- or second-hand.

Plants come in many sizes. One of the California big trees is the largest living thing on Earth, but some **algae** are so tiny that you need a powerful microscope to see them. Each plant has a size and shape that suit it for some special way of life. It took thousands of millions of years for plants to evolve into the types we see around us today. Scientists know this from fossilized plant remains preserved in ancient rocks.

The primitive salt-water stromatolites.

The first plants

The first plant-like organisms seem to have lived in the sea, perhaps 3,000 million years ago. Probably they sprang from tiny 'germs' resembling some bacteria alive today. Unlike their ancestors, these plant-like organisms contained the green substance **chlorophyll.** Chlorophyll helps green plants use the energy in sunlight to manufacture foods from the simple chemicals in air and water. At the same time green plants give off the gas oxygen as waste.

These first plant-like living things were the **blue-greens** or cyanophytes. Some may have formed filmy mats in ponds, as blue-greens do today. Others built hard, limy cushions called stromatolites on the floors of shallow salt-water bays. Off the coast of north-west Australia you can see living stromatolites like those that thrived more than 2,000 million years ago.

Blue-greens and those other lowly water plants such as algae must have moisture to survive. You might guess this for yourself if you have seen what happens to the algae known as seaweeds, when they lie stranded on a shore. On land they just dry up and die.

Plants invade the land

The first land plants may have been algae growing as a green scum along the moist rims of ponds and rivers. By 400 million years ago plants had developed that were better able to invade the land. Some gained a waxy outer surface to stop their moist insides from drying out. They also produced stiff stems that raised them up toward the light. Plant juices flowed up or down through tubes inside their stems, to carry nourishment from one part of the plant to another. Early land plants like *Cooksonia* were little more than branching stems crowned by hollow caps, producing tiny

Swamp-like forests flourished 300 million years ago.

spores from which new plants might grow.

Soon, though, came plants with roots to suck up water, and leaves for making food. Some of these prehistoric plants had strong woody fibres in their stems and grew into the world's first trees. There were giant horsetails 10.5 metres high (35 feet), and mighty scale trees like *Lepidodendron* three times as tall as that. (Its living relatives today are mosses low enough for you to tread on.) Huge scale trees, giant horsetails, ferns and other plants formed vast forests on warm, low-lying shores.

Plants with seeds

In time, the wet lands dried up. New kinds of trees with more effective ways of reproducing took over from the ancient giants. Their lives had begun as tiny unprotected spores scattered on moist soil. The new trees grew from seeds that had been nourished and protected on the parent plants; these trees invaded lands away from open water.

The first main group of seed plants to appear are known as **gymnosperms** or 'naked seed' plants. Among these were the **conifers** whose seeds develop within protective cones. There were also ginkgoes, with strange, flat, fan-shaped leaves. Tough-leaved gymnosperms began to spread up hillsides.

Later still came flowering plants, whose seeds were protected by an outer fruit. These flowering plants are also called **angiosperms,** which roughly means 'cased seeds'. Angiosperms include all familiar farm and garden plants. They range from trees over 100 metres high (328 feet) to floating duckweeds only a few millimetres across.

Flowering plants proved enormously successful. By 60 million years ago they were replacing gymnosperms. In time angiosperms invaded almost every kind of land and climate. Today, flowering plants of one kind or another are the most plentiful of all plants, whether in deserts, grasslands, broadleaved forests or on the farms carved out of the forests. Angiosperms even thrive in water and cold polar lands. But gymnosperms still rule in northern forests. And all around the world you still find algae, ferns, lichens, mosses and other lowly ancient kinds of plant.

These cycads, growing in South Africa, are the most primitive gymnosperms alive today. They have not changed their shape over millions of years.

Water plants

Salty seas and freshwater rivers, lakes and swamps all have their special kinds of plant. Each kind is adapted to cope with the conditions where it lives.

The open sea

If you dip an empty bottle in the sea, the water that flows in may hold tens of millions of plants so small that you need a microscope to see them. In cool seas most will be the minute organisms called **diatoms** and **flagellates.** Under a micro-scope a diatom looks like a tiny blob of jelly in a glassy pillbox. Diatoms come in up to 20,000 kinds—some rodlike, others shaped as discs. Many have corners with projecting spines.

In warm seas flagellates far outnumber diatoms. Some flagellates look like Chinese hats, others resemble pots, clubs or balloons on strings. They all lash them-selves along with one or two tiny whiplike

Below *Several types of diatoms.*

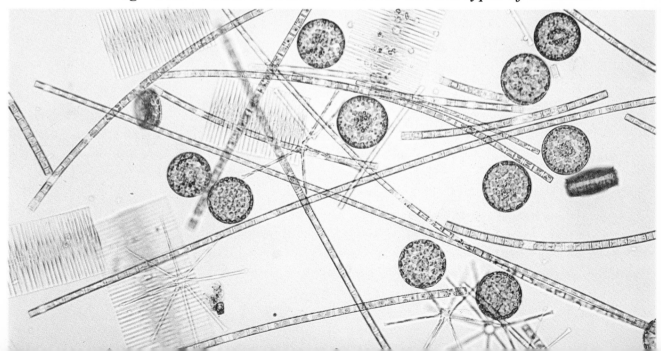

Labels on image: giant kelp, oar weed, sugar kelp, bladder wrack, sea lettuce, serrated wrack

threads. Indeed the name flagellate means 'whip-bearer'.

Diatoms and flagellates are the most plentiful organisms in the mass of tiny plants that drift about in the surface waters of the seas. Such drifting plants are known as **phytoplankton.** Phytoplankton cannot live in the dark sunless depths, for down there the plants cannot get light to give them energy for making food.

Left Some flagellates group together into spheres called *volvox.*

Above Seaweeds growing at different depths.

Coastal plants

Many plants thrive in shallow coastal waters or on the shore itself. Rocky shores are homes to seaweeds. Some are flimsy, others rubbery or hard. Their long fronds are held up by and take nourishment from the surrounding water. Meanwhile their root-like 'holdfasts' grip underwater boulders so hard that only the fiercest storms can dislodge them. The green seaweeds need bright light, so these grow only in shallow water. Brown seaweeds can thrive lower down. Red seaweeds need least light of all. Their feathery fronds or brittle stems flourish in the shade cast by rocks or brown weeds overhead. The largest seaweed is giant kelp, a strap-like brown seaweed long enough to wrap around a house.

Sheltered estuaries with floors of soft, fine mud are home to several kinds of

Above *The stilt-like roots of the mangrove take oxygen from the air.*

Below *The fleshy leaves of glasswort appear as the tide goes out.*

flowering plants. Underwater meadows of dark green eelgrass grow on the lower shore. Higher up, the falling tide reveals bunches of glasswort. Their fleshy finger-like leaves store water when the tide has fallen, and can survive in salty air. Cord grass grows here too. Its stiff stems trap mud. Such plants help to raise mud above the level of the sea. As the mud dries out, land plants start moving in. On warm, tropical muddy shores, mangroves are the plant invaders. These trees throw down stilt-like roots from branches, or else sprout roots with 'knees' that jut out above the mud. Either way, the roots take the oxygen they need from the air, for there is little oxygen in mud.

Shore plants can also anchor shifting sands and pebbles. Tall marram grass sprouts on sand dunes—the sandy hummocks formed where wind has

Below *Clumps of sea kale flourishing above the high-tide mark.*

Above *A typical variety of freshwater plants.*

blown sands up the beach. Sea kale and sea holly manage to put down their roots among the stones of shingle shores.

Freshwater plants

These grow most abundantly in lowland waters, for they are usually richest in the dissolved minerals that plants need.

Different plants grow best in different stretches of a river. Few can put down roots in the fast-flowing water of a mountain stream. But lower down, the

13

current flows more slowly; water crow-foot sprouts from sands that have settled on the river bed. A slow-flowing lowland stretch of river has most plants of all. Flags, water-lilies and others grow in the soft rich silt that forms the river bank or bed. These plants also thrive in the muddy beds of ponds and lakes.

Only free-floating plants live in the deepest water of a lake. Water hyacinths are floaters that smother huge stretches of some lakes and rivers in the tropics. Submerged plants like hornwort and Canadian pondweed root near the lake rim. Reeds, horsetails and other 'marginals' rise from the muddy margin.

As mud and the dead, fallen leaves of water plants pile up on its floor, the lake or pond grows shallower. So marginal plants can grow ever farther from the old shore. In time a whole lake may become a reed **swamp.** As this grows drier still, small trees and bushes can invade. In this way, the swamp slowly becomes a **marsh,** and then a low, damp woodland. Lastly, taller trees move in. These processes of plant **succession** turn lakes and ponds into dry land.

Water hyacinths have nearly smothered this lake in Paraguay.

Plants in cold places

Only very hardy plants can survive among Earth's colder regions, in the high mountain peaks and polar lands of the far north and far south. Even in the hot tropics, thin mountain air holds little heat, so each night on a high peak is like a short sharp winter. Polar winters are long, dark and cold enough to kill most ordinary plants. In the short polar summers the sun may not set for months, yet soil just below the surface, known as **permafrost**, stays forever frozen. Thin, poor soil, and dry and chilling winds are other hazards.

Tundra plants grow close to the ground in the short summer.

Tundra plants

Despite all these problems, more than 800 kinds of flowering plants thrive in the far north, although only two flourish in the far south, for most of Antarctica is always under ice. All these plants grow in the polar region known as **tundra,** a word meaning 'treeless plain'. In winter the tundra is gripped by frost or buried under snow and ice, but when these melt they reveal a covering of small, low-growing plants.

Tough lichens and mosses cling to naked rocks. Heath plants like crowberries and bilberries carpet drier soils. Sedges grow on lower ground. Here and there rise grassy hummocks, while birch and willow trees no higher than a man's waist sprout from damp depressions, and there are mossy **bogs.** In early summer, great stretches of the tundra turn a vivid green, splashed with the bright blooms of flowers like anemones, gentians, Iceland poppies and saxifrages.

Beating the cold

Somehow all tundra plants survive the bitter winters. In very cold weather, the sap in any ordinary plant would freeze and burst its cell walls, in the same way as ice bursts water pipes in a house. But the sap of many Arctic plants contains a kind of antifreeze that stops this happening. Lichens and mosses turn brittle with the cold as they cling to barren rocks, yet these lowly plants do not actually die.

Then, too, many polar plants escape the worst effects of winter because they grow so low that a covering of snow protects them from the harshest frosts. Low-growing plants are also the safest from the harsh winds that tend to dry out the moisture in their leaves, which the plants cannot replenish because the ground is frozen. Some polar plants guard their moisture by having leaves with waxy leakproof surfaces. The Arctic poppy's hairy stems trap a layer of still air and so keep winds at bay. Seeds may endure long spells of cold underground. Arctic lupin seeds have been said to sprout after being frozen for 10,000 years. Tender buds also bide their time, protected from the worst cold beneath the soil, or hidden in a mass of leaves.

But many of the tender shoots that rise

The hairy stems of the tiny arctic poppy protect the plant from icy winds.

A cushion of purple saxifrage.

above the snow are likely to be struck and killed by whizzing, windblown grains of snow, sand or gravel.

Slow growers

Plants grow very slowly in the polar cold. Some lichens that spread like stains over the rocks could be 4,000 years old. But flowering plants make the most of the short summer growing season.

Most flowering tundra plants can make new leaves when the air would be too cold for other, more tender plants to grow. Many have dark leaves or dark-hued petals that absorb more heat from the sun than pale ones would. Purple saxifrage and mountain avens form tight-packed cushions that hug the ground. Such cushion plants break the force of the wind and trap heat in their centres. The inside of a cushion plant may be twice as warm as the surrounding air.

Many plants grow out sideways instead of upwards, to dodge the winter winds. Dwarf willows reach only waist

A dwarf willow protects itself from the cold by growing over a rock.

height yet throw out branches six metres (20 feet) long. Their roots grow sideways too: no tundra plant could thrust roots down into the permafrost.

In summer, brightly coloured petals attract flies and insects that fertilize the flowers' seeds. But plants in polar soils take years to grow from seed. Instead, many new plants start as shoots sprouting from the ends of runners thrown out by a parent plant.

Edelweiss flowers trap heat with their hairy petals.

Mountain plants

The higher you climb up a mountain, the colder and thinner the air becomes. Even on the equator, at night or on a cloudy day the highest peaks can be as cold as a polar winter and up there winds blow fiercely. The plants on these high mountain peaks cope with these problems much as tundra plants do. In places, dwarf willows, birches or conifers sprout branches that scramble over the ground. The cobweb houseleek and the edelweiss, found in the Alps, grow hairy coverings that trap heat and stop moisture escaping. Mountain crowfoot even produces 'antifreeze' sap. The strange giant lobelias and groundsels of high African peaks trap heat in rosettes of tightly packed leaves. *Soldanella* is a little alpine flower that actually gives off heat—enough to melt the snow above. In spring its flowers peep out of snow slopes in the Alps.

What grows on any mountain depends upon three things: height, amount of moisture, and distance from the equator. Even at the equator, only hardy lichens and mosses grow on the bare rocks of the highest peaks. Lower down, crumbled rocks give rootholds for tough grasses. In the Alps you find mountain meadows, brightened in spring by blooms of anemones, alpine buttercups, carnations, pinks, gentians, heathers and rhododendrons. Lower down, if it is moist enough, you may find forests of conifers—needle-leaved trees like pines and spruces. On the even warmer, lowest slopes broadleaved trees thrive.

People sometimes say that if you climb a mountain on the equator you pass through all the main kinds of vegetation you would find if you journeyed at sea level from the equator to the Arctic. This is not exactly true, but the plants you find up a mountain do differ greatly according to the height at which they grow.

Right *Giant groundsel and lobelia plants growing high on Mt. Kenya, Africa.*

Vegetation regions of the world

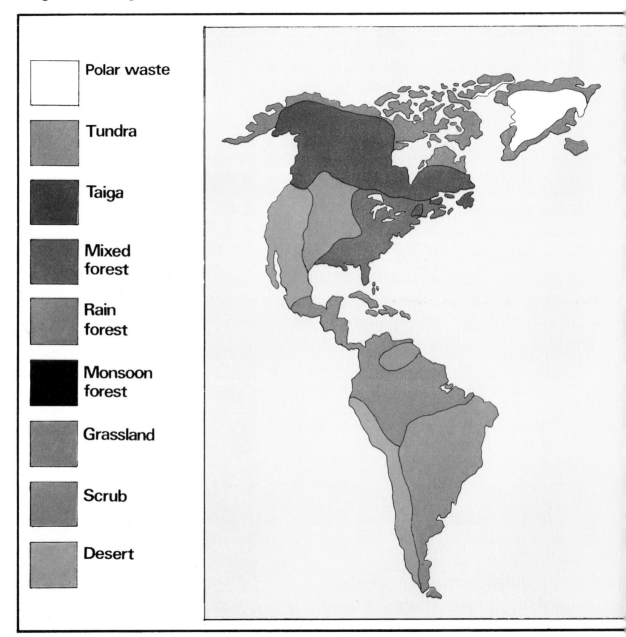

Polar waste

Tundra

Taiga

Mixed forest

Rain forest

Monsoon forest

Grassland

Scrub

Desert

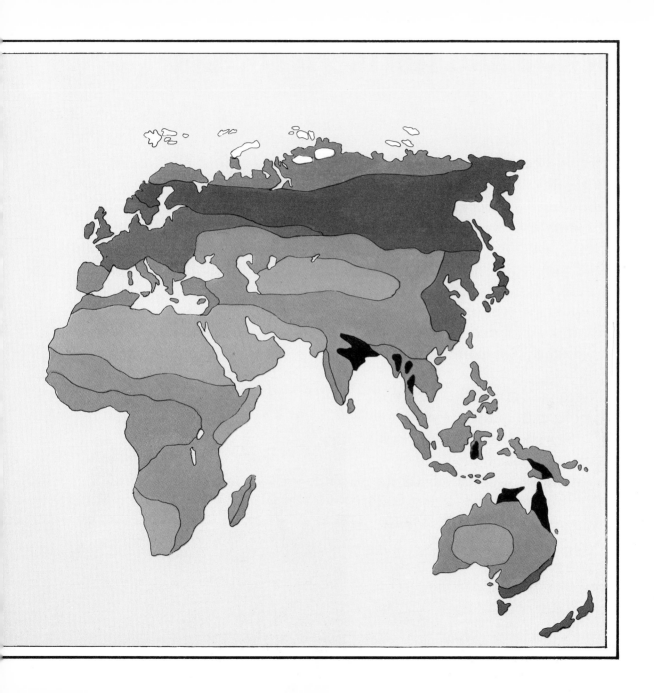

Temperate and northern forests

Forests sprawl over immense regions of the northern continents (see pages 22-23). The world's greatest forest belt is mostly made of coniferous (cone-bearing) trees. This forest forms a broad band across northern North America, Europe and northern Asia just south of the tundra. Geographers call this northern forest belt the **taiga.** Here grow **evergreen** conifers such as firs, pines and spruces, but there are far fewer kinds of tree than flourish in the tropics.

South of the taiga, parts of the northern continents are mostly under flowering broadleaved trees—kinds like beeches, oaks and maples, that shed their leaves in winter. These **deciduous,** or leaf-shedding trees, get their name from the Latin word *decidere* which means 'to fall off'. Deciduous trees once formed great forests, but most of these have been chopped down. Now scattered woods remain in the east of North America, Europe and East Asia. In the southern hemisphere, though, Chile and New Zealand have forests of the southern beech.

Each kind of forest thrives best in a particular kind of climate. Conifers flourish mostly in climates too cool for most broadleaved trees. This is why you also find coniferous forests on cool mountainsides in warmer climates.

The taiga

Conifers flourish in the taiga because they can survive the long, cold winters there.

The evergreen taiga forest.

Snow cannot break these branches.

Many conifers have sloping sides and slim pointed leaves like needles. Snow slides off their springy branches instead of piling up until it snaps them off. Fierce winds do little damage, for air slips easily between the tough, narrow leaves. These leaves are made in ways that help them to endure intense cold. In winter they lose some moisture and change in other ways that help to stop them freezing, for that would make the leaf cells burst and kill the leaves. Many conifers are also rich in sticky resin which oozes from a damaged trunk or branch to seal the wound.

But the ways in which their leaves and wood are made produce problems for the forest plants. The acid in the conifers' tough leaves and the resin in their timber slow down the rate at which these rot when they have fallen to the ground. This means that tiny organisms in the soil cannot easily break down the leaves and wood into nutrients that help other plants to grow. So a thick layer of dead needle-like leaves covers the forest floor. But down there the trees find hidden helpers: a mass of growing threads belonging to the non-green

Toadstools and lichen growing on a conifer forest floor.

plant-like organisms called **fungi.** Fungi help to rot dead leaves and wood, and release their minerals. Tree roots can then suck up these minerals, which help to make new wood and leaves.

Few plants grow in the poor taiga soils, beneath the trees. But bog plants thrive where soil is waterlogged, and sandy soils are homes to heathers, orchids and mosses. In autumn, too, brightly coloured toadstools sprout from the fungal threads growing underground or hidden in decaying wood.

Deciduous woods and forests

Deciduous trees like chestnuts, oaks and maples grow in temperate regions—lands with winters milder than those the northern conifers endure. But even temperate lands may suffer winter gales and frosts. Shedding leaves before cold weather starts helps these trees survive. A leafless oak cannot have its leaves torn off by gales or killed by drought. (In winter its broad, soft leaves would lose more water to air than they could gain from soil, because the soil is so cold that the roots cannot suck up moisture.)

Deciduous trees shed leaves to a plan. First, the dying leaves change colour. This is because their green chlorophyll decays, releasing yellow, red or orange substances. By the time the leaves fall, a corky layer has sealed each scar left where a leaf stalk drops off its twig. Meanwhile the twigs have sprouted buds containing next year's leaves. Concentrated juices in these buds help to stop them freezing, and many buds have an outer covering of hairy scales. These stop harsh winds sucking moisture from the tender leaves within.

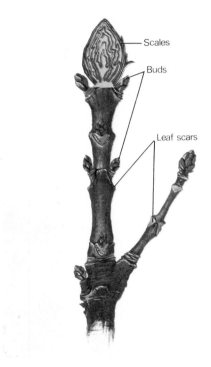

Scales

Buds

Leaf scars

Inside a wood

The floors of deciduous woods contain more kinds of plants than you find growing under conifers. This is largely because the soil is rich in plant foods made from rotted leaves. Below tall oaks or other forest trees grow lesser trees such as holly. Lower still come shrubs. In spring, the floor of many a European

Woodland flowers: daffodils, primroses and wood anemones.

wood gleams with the flowers of soft-stemmed **herbaceous** plants such as

27

bluebells, lesser celandines, primroses, violets and wood anemones. Some plants of this low herbaceous layer spend most of the year underground as bulbs. When winter ends they push up leaves and flowers toward the bright light that shines down between the bare tree branches above. When the trees sprout leaves the light grows dimmer and the bulbous plants die back. But dim light is enough for the mosses that form the lowest plant layer in the wood. Lowly mosses, ferns and lichens also grow higher up on trunks and branches.

Trees that break the rules

Not all broadleaved flowering trees that grow in temperate climates shed their leaves each winter. Cork oaks and certain other broadleaved trees are evergreen. They thrive near the Mediterranean Sea and in other lands with mild, rainy winters and hot, dry summers (see pages 22-23). The leaves' tough, shiny surfaces help to stop moisture escaping in the rainless months. Between the trees, or where these trees have been felled, grow tough-leaved shrubs that also beat the summer drought.

Similarly, not all conifers have narrow leaves and not all of them keep their leaves all year. The kauri pine and monkey-puzzle from the southern hemisphere are broad-leaved conifers; and the larches found in northern forests shed all their leaves each winter.

The monkey puzzle—a broadleaved conifer.

Tropical forests

Tropical **rain forests** are among the warmest, wettest places on Earth. They sprawl over lowlands close to the equator in South America, West and Central Africa, and South East Asia. Rain falls almost every day, washing plant foods deep down into the soil where they are lost for ever. Yet plants sprout quickly from the warm, wet, reddish soil. Their shallow roots suck nourishment from the fallen, rotted leaves and wood that thinly coat the forest floor. Indeed, more kinds of plant grow here than anywhere on Earth. As many as one hundred kinds of tree—some huge—occur in just one hectare (2.4 acres).

Forest giants

Many tropical rain forest trees are vast. Some grow more than 50 metres (164 feet) high with massive trunks that soar like pillars in some great cathedral. Plank-like buttress roots, as high as a house, slope outward from each lower trunk to help support its colossal weight. The first branches sprout out high above the floor of the forest.

Most trees appear to be evergreen, shedding their broad leaves a few at a time as these grow old. Because there are no cold seasons, different trees of the same kind may flower and fruit at any time of year. Indeed, on the same tree some branches may bear flowers while others are producing fruits.

The buttressed trunk of a rain forest tree.

Palm trees grow in tropical rain forests everywhere, but each forest region has special types of tree. Sapele and ebony grow in Africa. Mahogany and greenheart come from South America. *Santiria* is a tree that thrives in South East Asia. There are hundreds more.

The layered forest

If you could climb one of the tallest trees in a tropical rain forest you would pass through five distinct plant layers.

First comes the herb layer, up to 2

The layers of a rain forest.

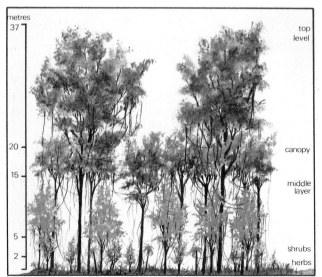

metres (6.5 feet) high. Here, on the shady forest floor, you find plants such as arums, ferns, or African violets. Some forest-floor plants have reddish leaves. These help to make the most of the dim light that filters down from above. Herbaceous plants grow fairly far apart, except where light is strong in clearings or by streams. But fungi grow on rotting vegetation anywhere because they need no light at all.

Next comes the shrub layer, 2 to 5 metres (6.5 to 16.4 feet) high. Shrubs thrive here, also palms and tiny trees holding up their leaves toward the light.

Higher still you reach the middle layer. This is made up of the leafy crowns of short trees. The crowns' long, slim shapes help to soak up the soft light slanting downward through the leaves above.

The fourth layer contains the spreading crowns of the tall forest trees. Their lower leaves are always bathed by moist, warm air. Many of these leaves are large and thin, and end in drooping points that let rain drip off to the ground. By comparison the topmost leaves are often leathery. A tough 'skin' helps them to survive the drier, hotter air above. The trees' crowns touch to form a canopy; from above it looks like a sea of green splashed with colour where flowers bloom or ripe fruits hang.

The highest level consists of the scattered crowns of the very tallest trees, which stand up above the rest.

Plants growing on other plants

Tropical rain forest plants seem to jostle one another in their bid to reach bright sunlight high above. Woody climbers called *lianas* cling to tree trunks as their rope-like stems grow rapidly to the very tops of trees. Some are 240 metres (787 feet) long and as thick as a man's thigh. One type, called a strangling fig, sprouts on and around trees until it suffocates them. But *lianas* have plant enemies too. The stinking corpse lily of Malaysia is a **parasite** that sucks sap from their roots. This leafless plant produces the world's largest flower, whose smell of rotting flesh attracts the flies that spread its pollen.

Plants called **epiphytes** reach light by rooting in the soil lodged in cracks high up on trees. The cheese plants, bromeliads and orchids often kept as house plants in cooler climates all grow wild as epiphytes on forest trees.

Lianas festoon the forest like ropes.

South American mist forest.

Monsoon and other forests

Not all forests in the tropics are the same. Rain forests only flourish where water is plentiful all the year. In monsoon lands, where some months are dry, the forest trees shed their leaves before the drought sets in. Best known of these is the teak. This mighty timber tree from Indian and South East Asian **monsoon forests** sheds all its leaves in the dry season. New shoots appear only when the monsoon rains begin. Other types of deciduous trees also thrive in the drier, more open, forest lands of South America and Africa.

Very different again are the **mist forests** found in the cool cloud that covers certain mountains in the tropics. Here there is just one forest layer and the trees do not grow very tall. But their trunks and branches wear thick coats of epiphytic plants: ferns, lichens, liverworts and mosses all flourish in the misty, saturated air.

Another type of vegetation grows where farmers or foresters have burned or chopped down tropical rain forest. Rain washes many nutrients from the bare soil. No big trees can grow. Instead their place is taken by a tangled mass of undergrowth called **jungle.** Travellers can walk freely across the open floor of a rain forest, but they have to hack their way through dense jungle vegetation. Rain forests may not regrow for hundreds of years, if ever.

The grasslands

In some parts of the world a sea of grass and other soft-stemmed plants stretches in all directions as far as you can see. Grassy plains cover vast areas of the tropics, and inland regions of lands with cooler climates. Here, rain falls mostly in one season only. When rain arrives the land turns green and bright with flowers. As drought or cold sets in, plants die and the land turns brown and parched. Some grassland soils are just too dry for trees. And even where these sprout, many die in fires that sweep the countryside. Other seedling trees get bitten off and killed by grazing animals.

How grasses grow

Grasses grow in ways that help them to survive being nibbled, dried or chilled. The leaves grow upward from stems that

A huge stretch of grassland on the South Island of New Zealand.

mostly hug the ground. When a grazing animal bites the top off a young leaf, it just regrows from the base. But tall, old leaves cannot regrow in this way. These grasses may get trampled, but this damage simply makes them send out side-stems, on or just below the ground. New roots and leaves spring from the bulging joints along these stems. In this way a mass of close-packed stems will produce a big grassy tussock or the kind of dense, springy carpet known as turf.

Annual grasses produce tiny flowers.

Grasses that only live a year push up a flower-head from each stem. Windblown pollen fertilizes the grass seeds. These then drop off and survive the dry months lying in or on the soil. Longer lived grasses push up fewer flower-heads in the growing season. But they do produce tender shoots that live on through the drought, protected by the sheaths of old, dead leaves.

Tropical grasslands

Tropical grasslands sprawl over more than one-third of Africa, where they are called **savannah.** Savannah also covers parts of India and northern Australia. Similar countryside occurs in South America where it goes by the Spanish names *campos* and *llanos.* Tropical grasslands tend to have a short rainy 'summer', a long dry winter and then a spell of intense dry heat.

Tall, coarse grasses flourish here. In moist places Africa's elephant grasses grow more than twice as high as a man. Isolated trees rise here and there—the African savannah is dotted with acacia trees. Sharp thorns help to protect their feathery leaves from browsing animals,

A huge baobab tree in the savannah of Botswana, Africa.

and many acacias shed their leaves to survive drought. Africa and Australia are also homes of baobabs—trees which store water in mighty trunks that bulge like barrels.

Somehow, savannah trees and grasses survive the fires that often burn the land when grass is dead and brittle. Dead leaf-sheaths help to protect the young grass shoots from the fire. Red oat-grass seeds survive by burrowing: daily changes in the amount of moisture in the air make the fallen seeds screw their way into the soil, where they lie safely out of reach of flames. Many savannah trees have a thick, corky, fire-resistant bark.

Temperate grasslands

These lie mostly in the dry hearts of continents outside the tropics. The two largest temperate grassland areas are the North American **prairies,** and the **steppes** which stretch 4,000 kilometres (2,500 miles) from western Russia into southwest Siberia. Argentina's **pampas,** South Africa's **veld** and Australia's **downlands** are temperate grasslands in the southern continents.

Much of the world's temperate grassland is very hot in summer and intensely cold in winter, and mostly has little rain. Grasses here are shorter than those growing in the tropics, and trees are very few indeed. But which types of grasses grow varies with the local climate. Fairly tall grass thrives in North America's rather moist eastern prairies. Shorter grasses flourish in the drier middle prairies. Very short wiry grasses form separated clumps in the western prairies —the driest part of all. In the same way, the driest pampas are little more than

The tussocky pampas of Bolivia, South America.

desert, yet tall tussocky grasses sprout in the moister, eastern pampas.

In spring and early summer, temperate grasslands are brightened by the flowers of clovers and other members of the pea family, and plant foods produced by organisms living in their roots enrich the soil. From May to June the steppes are alive with red and yellow tulips, anemones, irises, dark-red peonies and the blue of flowering sage. Some flowering plants survive the drought and winter cold because they are hardy shrubs, or have underground bulbs, swollen stems or roots.

Man-made grasslands

People once thought that the world's great grasslands had formed where it was too dry for trees to grow. A study of pre-history proves this is wrong. Much of Africa's savannah is moist enough for forest trees to grow. Indeed, long ago, open forest probably flourished there. Similarly, open woodland may have covered much of what are now the treeless steppes and prairies.

In all these places great changes have

Grazing livestock prevents scrub from growing back on to grassland.

been brought about by Man. Early Man learned that burning off the forest increased the spread of grasses, and encouraged the large, wild grazing animals which he hunted. Later, when Man had learned to herd animals, burning off old grasses encouraged fresh, young growth to feed and fatten the flocks. Today, even the steppe and prairie grasses have been largely replaced by cultivated grasses such as wheat, oats, maize and barley.

Western Europe and much of eastern North America lost their forests in the last few centuries. Once woodsmen had chopped down the trees, farmers and shepherds moved in with their cattle, ploughs and sheep. Today farm animals graze on man-made pastures. Even the kinds of grasses grown are sown deliberately. From the 7,500 known kinds of grass, farmers choose only from the three dozen or so quick-growing types that thrive in spite of heavy grazing. But where these pastures have been left ungrazed, scrub and trees move in again.

Plants that beat the drought

If you divided the Earth's land into a hundred parts, at least fifteen of them would be desert. Great belts of desert cover south-west North America and sprawl from northern Africa through Arabia and on to eastern Central Asia. Other deserts lie in western South America, south-west Africa and central Australia.

Ordinary plants would quickly shrivel up and die in deserts, for these lands are usually very dry. Some are also very hot. Rain rarely falls, and when it does the heat of the sun quickly sucks up moisture from the surface. No plants can root in deserts floored by solid rock or shifting sand. Yet desert plants manage to flourish in some places—beating the drought in one way or another.

Resisting drought

Desert plants that survive the long dry months are known as drought resisters. Many have strange shapes that help them to exist in spite of the lack of rain.

The best-known drought resisters are the juicy plants called **succulents.** Among these are the cacti from North and South America, and many African spurges. These look like cacti, but unlike cacti they do not sprout hairs or spines in tufts. Both plants suck up rainwater from shallow

Typical drought resistant plants.

Desert plants

yucca

barrel cactus

prickly pear

38

roots that spread out far in all directions. The tree-like saguaro cactus of Arizona towers 15 metres (50 feet); the roots sprawl over the same distance, but nowhere are they more than a few centimetres (or inches) deep. When rain falls, these shallow-rooted succulents capture the moisture before it evaporates.

The plants store the water in their fleshy stems, which swell up as they fill with moisture. After rain, a big saguaro weighing 10 tonnes contains 9 tonnes of water. Some cacti are shaped like pleated barrels, and the pleats open out as water swells the stem. In a long drought the stem shrinks and its pleats draw closer together.

Succulents suck up water in just a few hours, but they can store it in their stems for months. This is largely because they do not lose it through their leaves, like ordinary plants. Cacti and desert spurges have leaves so small that you may not even notice them. Their green stems do the work of making food instead of leaves. A prickly pear's stems even look like thick, flat leaves, joined end to end. The stems are waterproofed by waxy substances that stop their moisture leaking out. Water cannot readily escape through the plants' tiny breathing pores because these close during the hot daylight hours. They open only in the cool night air, when little water will evaporate.

Desert oddities

Most desert shrubs sprout leaves only when it rains, and shed them again when the drought sets in. But mesquites keep their leaves all the year. Their roots burrow as much as 30 metres (98 feet) to seek water from a year-round store deep down beneath the surface. Other plants that flourish all the year include the yuccas, also of America. Most yuccas form low shrubs with leaves like stiff, green swords jutting from a fibrous trunk, but the Joshua tree rises nearly 10 metres (33 feet) above the desert floor, with branching stems that end in leaves arranged as spiky tufts.

Few desert plants have leaves and buds that can be shrivelled by the drought and still revive. The North American creosote bush is one exception. In dry months creosote bushes lose one quarter of their moisture

The Joshua tree manages to thrive in the Nevada Desert, USA.

and look dead, but come alive next time it rains. Creosote bushes spread outward very slowly from a parent plant. At least one cluster of such bushes is 11,700 years old. Creosote bushes seem to be the oldest living things on Earth.

Even stranger drought resisters live in south-west Africa. The little plants known as 'living stones' produce two swollen fleshy leaves that look like pebbles. The miracle plant, *Welwitschia,* sprouts two huge split leaves. These sprawl out raggedly about 3 metres (10 feet) from a central stem only a few centimetres high.

Prickly plants

A number of drought-resistant desert plants go armed with hard, sharp spikes. Thorns stick out from their stems, leaves or even from the fruits. The ocotillo's thorns are really the mid-ribs of leaves that died off when the last drought started.

Thorns help to protect some plants from being munched by browsing animals. Also they trap some dew, which then drops to the ground, where the roots can suck it up.

The curious two-leaved Welwitschia *plant.*

Dodging the drought

While some plants endure the desert drought others avoid it altogether. Some fast-growing **annuals** die off, leaving only seeds behind. These lie hidden in the ground through rainless months, or even years. Some contain special chemicals which stop them sprouting until heavy rain has soaked the ground and washed the chemicals away. Then the seeds sprout quickly. The African plant *Boerhaavia repens* can grow from seed and make seeds of its own in just eight days. Many other desert annuals of the poppy, pea and daisy families scatter seed a fortnight after sprouting. While they grow, a mass of blossom hides the dusty desert floor. At times like this

The brilliant but short-lived Sturt's desert pea.

Australian deserts gleam bright red with the flowers of Sturt's desert pea.

But desert annuals lead short lives: as the drought returns they are already withering.

Man and deserts

Where water can be brought or found, farmers grow crops in the desert. Rice, date palms and other plants thrive in the fertile strips and patches called oases, mostly near wells and rivers. Israeli farmers have even planted fruit trees in dry desert soil. They pile stones around the bottoms of the trunks. Dew forms on the stones at night and trickles down, providing water for the roots. In such ways man can make some deserts fertile.

But fertile land is also giving way to desert, where goats and cattle are allowed to eat all trees and pasture. South of Africa's Sahara Desert, scrawny desert plants invade lands where trees used to flourish.

Man affects the type of plants which grow in many regions of the world. Unless he takes great care, desert vegetation may swallow up great grasslands and forests of the tropics.

Man has learnt to cultivate crops nearthe desert oases.

Facts and figures

There are various estimates as to how much of the land is under various types of vegetation. Possibly 15 per cent is desert, 25 per cent semi-desert and grassland, 30 per cent forest, and the remaining 30 per cent is under cultivated plants and other vegetation.

The first-known plant-like organisms may have been the blue-greens, which appeared more than 2,000 million years ago.

The first land plants were simple plants like *Cooksonia,* which appeared by 400 million years ago. These were followed by seed plants, which were spreading by 350 million years ago. Conifers appeared 180 million years ago. Flowering plants were spreading fast by 60 million years ago.

One estimate gives the total number of living plant species at 300,000.

The largest plant in the world is the California big tree. A single tree weighs over 2000 tonnes (2200 US tons), or ten times more than the largest animal—the blue whale.

The tallest trees are coast redwoods and certain types of eucalyptus, which can reach heights over 110 metres (360 feet).

Some grass plants can each produce root systems measuring more than 500 kilometres (315 miles).

In the course of one day, a tree such as the beech may suck up water equal to five times the weight of its leaves.

The fastest-growing plant is the giant grass called bamboo, which can grow up to 41 centimetres (16 inches) in a day.

Polar lichens are the slowest-growing plants. Some take 4,000 years to cover a patch of rock. They are also the hardiest plants, and are found growing on mountains near the South Pole.

The highest flowering plant grows in the Himalayas, at a height of around 6,000 metres (20,000 feet).

The small Arctic willow is the world's northernmost flowering plant. The southernmost flowering plant is a carnation found in Antarctica.

The oldest forests are the tropical rain forests, some of which are many millions of years old. The northern forests were killed off for a time by the last Ice Age.

Tropical rain forest also contains the greatest variety of tree species—over one hundred species per hectare (about 2.5 acres). This is four times as many as in even a species-rich temperate forest.

About 25,000 species of plant are at risk of being destroyed, and up to 200 species of flowering plants become extinct each year.

The destruction of tropical forest is currently taking place at an annual rate of some 6 to 20 million hectares (15 to 49 million acres).

Glossary

Algae are simple plants found in the sea, in fresh water, and on damp land. They include the seaweeds.

Annuals These are plants which complete their life cycle in one year.

Angiosperms are the flowering plants. Their seeds develop in a protective case known as a fruit.

Blue-green (cyanophyte) This simple organism contains chlorophyll and was once thought to be related to green algae, but it is now known to be more primitive than those plants.

Bogs are stretches of wet, spongy ground covered with rotting moss and other plants.

Chlorophyll is a green pigment found in plants. It helps them to use energy in sunlight to make foods from water and the gas carbon dioxide. This process is called photosynthesis.

Conifers are trees which produce their seeds in cones. They include cedars, firs, pines, spruces, and larches. Most evergreens, with narrow leaves. All conifers are gymnosperms.

Deciduous means 'leaf shedding'. Deciduous trees shed leaves before cold or dry seasons.

Diatoms are tiny plants made of a single cell, surrounded by a glassy wall. They belong to one group of algae.

Downlands Temperate grasslands in Australia and parts of southern England.

Epiphytes are plants that grow on others but do not use them as a source of food. Some lichens, mosses and orchids are epiphytes.

Evergreens Plants which bear leaves all the year round. They shed old leaves a few at a time, not all at once.

Flagellates are tiny organisms with 'whips' that help them to move through water. Some seem built more like animals than plants.

Fungi Simple plant-like organisms with no chlorophyll. They include moulds and mushrooms. Unlike green plants, fungi cannot make food. They feed on living substances, or their remains.

Gymnosperms are primitive seedplants. They include conifers, ginkgoes, and the palm-like cycads. Most of the last two kinds are extinct.

Herbaceous plants are those with soft and short-lived stems.

Jungle A tangled mass of plants which grows where tropical rain forest has been removed.

Marshes Stretches of soft wet land, sometimes under water.

Mist forest forms on mountain slopes that are usually covered in cloud.

Monsoon forest Fairly open tropical forest where rain falls mostly in one season.

Pampas are the flat, treeless, grassy plains of south-eastern South America.

Parasites live on other organisms and use them as a source of food. Mistletoe is a parasite.

Permafrost The ever-frozen subsoil of the tundra.

Phytoplankton are the plants in plankton.

Plankton describes the mostly tiny plants and animals that float or drift in the surface waters of the sea or a lake.

Prairies are the flat, treeless, grassy plains of North America.

Rain forest is the forest found in rainy climates. Tropical rain forests are among the largest forests in the world.

Savannah Tropical grassland. In South America the savannahs are called *llanos* and *campos*.

Steppes are the flat, treeless, grassy plains of eastern Europe and south-eastern South America.

Succession The series of changes in the kinds of plants growing on a piece of land. It starts with the first plants to encroach on it, and in time produces a fairly fixed variety of plants, called a climax.

Succulents are drought-resistant plants that store water in fleshy tissues. Cacti and houseleeks are two examples.

Swamps Stretches of low land, always under water and mostly overgrown with plants.

Taiga The great belt of coniferous forest growing south of the tundra.

Tundra A type of cold treeless plain found in Arctic lands.

Veld South Africa's high open grasslands and lower open countryside with scattered bushes.

Further reading

Green Worlds by David Bellamy (Aldus Books/Jupiter Books 1975)

Forest Life by Michael Boorer (Aldus Books/Jupiter Books 1975)

Jungles and People by G. Morgan (Wayland 1982)

Desert Life by J. Cloudsley-Thompson (Aldus Books/Jupiter Books 1975)

Deserts and People by J. Carson (Wayland 1982)

Grassland Life by Eric Duffey (Aldus Books/Jupiter Books 1975)

Grasslands and People by C. Horton (Wayland 1982)

Rivers and Lakes by P. Credland (The Danbury Press 1975)

Tundra and People by I. Barrett (Wayland 1982)

Polar Life by J. Lucas and S. Hayes (The Danbury Press 1975)

Atlas of Plant Life by Herbert Edlin (Heinemann 1973)

The Pictorial Encyclopedia of Plants and Flowers by F. A. Novak (Paul Hamlyn 1966)

Index

Picture acknowledgements

The illustrations in this book were provided by: Anthony Bannister/NHPA 8; H. Canter-Lund/NHPA 9; from Bruce Coleman Limited—Patrick Baker 5, J. S. Brownlie 42, Bruce Coleman 24, Eric Crichton 27, 28, Martin Dohrn 26, Michael Freeman 29, C. B. Frith 12 (above), Keith Gunnar 25, Udo Hirsch 12 (below), 36, Wayne Lankinen 15, 18, L. C. Marigo 14, Charlie Ott 40, Hans Reinhard 13, 20, 34, Alan Root 21, W. E. Ruth 33, John Shaw 4, Kim Taylor 10, G. Ziesler *cover*, 32; Stephen Dalton/NHPA 31; P. J. Greenhalf 13 (below); Ian Griffiths 43; HMSO Crown Copyright 6; Peter Johnson/NHPA 35; Jerg Kroener/NHPA 17, 19; K. H. Suritak 41; Wayland Picture Library 37. The diagrams on pages 11, 22-3, 27, 30, and 38 are by Bill Donohoe.